Amazing Life Cycles

BIRDS

John Allan

Emperor penguins live in the harsh conditions of the Antarctic. It is the father who will look after the egg and the young penguin, nursing it alone for 65 days.

Contents

Words that look **bold like this** are in the glossary.

ISBN 978-1-912108 077

First published in Great Britain in 2019 by
Hungry Tomato Ltd, The Old Bakery Studios, Blewetts Wharf,
Malpas Road, Truro, Cornwall, TR1 1QH, UK

Manufactured in the United States of America

What is a bird?

Water birds, such as ducks, have waterproof feathers.

Birds have something that no other animals have—feathers! Other animals have wings, and other animals lay eggs, but no other animals have feathers. A bird's feathers help to keep it warm.

Flying birds have stiff feathers that help them to fly. They have small, soft feathers called down for keeping warm.

Millions of years ago, dinosaurs lived on Earth. Dinosaurs were the **ancestors** of birds.

Birds lay eggs like **reptiles**, but birds are **endothermic** animals, like **mammals**.

Birds have scales on their legs and feet, and claws like reptiles.

Birds can be tiny, like the hummingbird in this picture, or huge like an ostrich below.

The ostrich is the biggest bird in the world. An adult male can be 8.2 feet (2.5 m) tall!

AMAZING BIRD FACT

An ostrich is too heavy to fly, but it can run fast. Its top speed is 43 mph (70 km/h).

Bird habitats

These swallows have built a nest in a garden shed!

A habitat is the place where a plant or an animal lives. Birds live in warm places, such as rainforests, and cold places, such as the Antarctic. Many birds live close to people, in cities or around farms.

Birds live in most of the world's habitats.

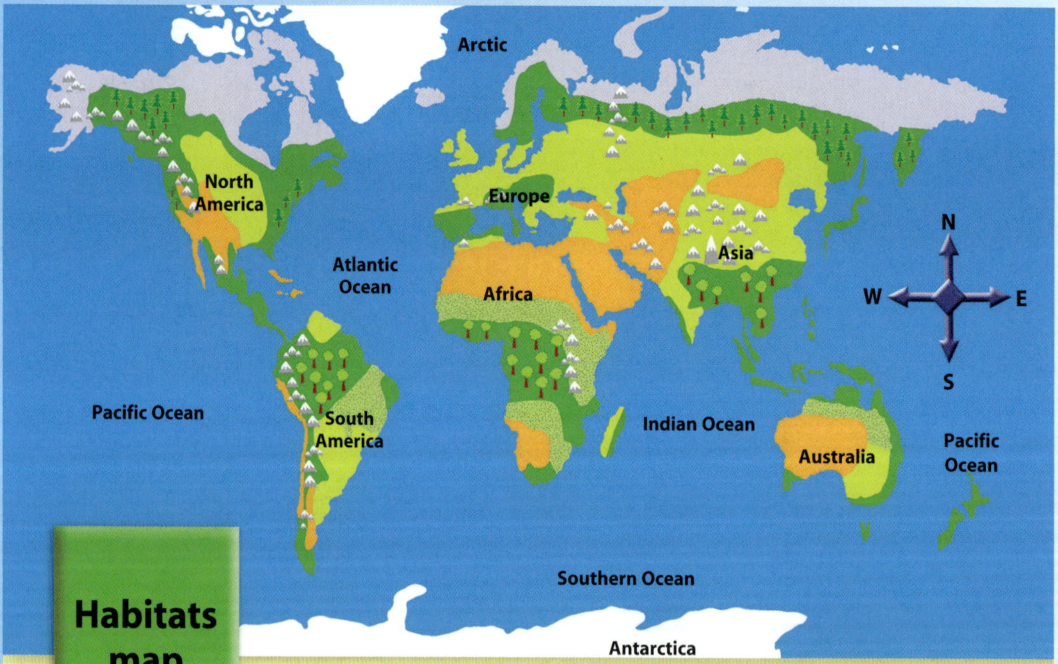

Map key

This map key shows you what the colours and pictures on the map mean.

- Temperate grasslands – areas that are dry in summer
- Tropical grasslands – hot, dry areas with few trees
- Tundra – cold, windy places
- Cool, rainy forests
- Arctic/Antarctica – frozen, snowy ground and icy seas
- Cold forests
- Warm, wet rainforest
- Deserts – dry land with little rain

Water-loving birds live beside rivers, lakes, or the sea. Gulls and other seabirds build their nests on cliffs. They gather together in big **colonies**.

This is an Atlantic Puffin colony.

Macaws live in warm rainforests.

Emperor penguins live in the Antarctic—the coldest place on Earth.

Emperor penguins are the biggest type of penguin.

A pair of wandering albatrosses.

Wings and flying

Birds have very light bodies. Their bones are* hollow *but very strong. Birds have powerful muscles to beat their wings up and down. Flying is hard work, so birds spend a lot of time eating.

The wandering albatross's wingspan is 3 feet (4 m).

The wandering albatross has the biggest **wingspan** in the bird kingdom. It spends most of its life flying over the ocean. It lands when it is time to **mate**, lay eggs, and raise its young.

AMAZING BIRD FACT

A robin's short wings are good for quick, short flights from place to place while catching bugs to eat.

This baby albatross is practicing flapping its wings.

Many baby birds fly without being shown how. They tumble out of the nest, spread their wings, and fly. Other babies need to practice.

Swifts catch insects in the air.

Buzzards fly high, looking out for food, such as mice, on the ground.

You can tell from a wing shape how a bird flies. A swift has long, pointed wings for fast flying.

A buzzard has broad wings for gliding and soaring high in the sky.

Mom meets dad

A male and a female swan pair for life.

Most birds* breed *every year, usually in the spring. Some birds stay together as a pair for life. Other birds have a new partner each year. Some females will have chicks with more than one male in the same year.

Peacock tail feathers are the longest feathers of any bird.

Some male birds have colorful feathers to attract females. The male peacock shows off to the female peahen by spreading his tail feathers like a fan.

Many male birds sing to attract a female to their **territory**. They defend their territory and their female by chasing away other males.

The male booby, spreads his wings and puts his beak in the air as part of his dance.

Some pairs of birds perform a dance together before they mate. The male blue-footed booby, dances for the female. He shows her his blue feet and whistles.

AMAZING BIRD FACT

To attract a mate the male frigate bird puffs out his bright red throat like a balloon.

This female blackbird is gathering material for her nest.

Eggs and nests

Many female birds make a nest on their own. Others are helped by their partner. Some birds make the nest before they mate—some do it after they mate. After it is made, the female bird lays her eggs in the nest.

Female birds sit on the eggs to keep them warm. This is called **incubation**. Some males help with this job too, and they bring food for the female.

The female stork lays up to four eggs in her nest.

The white stork's nest is made of sticks. The storks add more sticks every year, so the nest gets bigger and bigger!

This bald eagle is looking after her chicks

Chicks **hatch** from the eggs. Many chicks are helpless. Mom and dad bring food for the chicks to eat.

This great spotted woodpecker makes a nest in a hole in a tree.

Some birds make nests from grass, twigs, or leaves. The flamingo (above) makes a nest of mud with a hollow top. It will lay one or two eggs.

What is a life cycle?

A robin chick eats about 140 bugs, spiders, and worms a day!

1 An adult male and female bird meet and mate.

Life Cycle

6 When they are ready to go off on their own, the chicks leave the nest. Some parents teach their chicks how to fly. This is a picture of a young robin.

5 The parents bring the chicks food to eat. Some birds remove their chicks' poo from the nest, too!

A life cycle is all the different stages and changes that a plant or animal goes through in its life. This diagram shows the life cycle of a bird.

2 The female lays eggs in a nest.

Robin's live in Europe, North Africa, and parts of Asia.

# of a Bird

3 The female sits on the eggs to keep them warm. Some male birds bring the female food while she does this.

4 The eggs hatch. Many chicks are blind and have no feathers when they hatch.

AMAZING BIRD LIFE CYCLE

Hornbill

Hornbills live in the forests of Africa and Asia. The hornbill uses its large beak, or bill, to eat fruit, and to catch insects, lizards and snakes.

This is a southern ground hornbill. It feeds on the ground.

This great Indian hornbill lives in trees.

A female hornbill takes a last look before she blocks the nest entrance.

Most types of hornbill find their food in trees, but some feed on the ground.

Hornbills nest in holes in trees. The female lays her eggs, then shuts herself inside. She blocks the entrance with a wall made from droppings mixed with mud and squashed fruit.

LIFE CYCLE FACTS
The female hornbill lays up to six eggs. The chicks hatch in about 30 to 40 days.

The eggs hatch, but it may be three months before the female comes out. When the chicks get too big, she breaks open the wall and climbs out. The chicks stay in the hole until they are ready to fly.

The male hornbill passes the female food through a slit in the wall.

AMAZING BIRD LIFE CYCLE

Killdeer

Killdeers live on grasslands. They eat worms, beetles, grasshoppers, and snails. Killdeers nest on the ground where there are lots of dangers—chicks can run as soon as they hatch!

A killdeer will run at a horse or a cow to scare it and to stop the big animal from stepping on its eggs.

The killdeer's eggs are **camouflaged** to hide them from egg-eating **predators**.

Killdeer chicks have feathers as soon as they hatch.

On the grassland there is nowhere to hide. The chicks have to sit still in the grass.

To protect its family from predators, such as foxes, the killdeer has a trick. It drags one of its wings on the ground so it looks injured.

The fox follows the killdeer thinking it will get an easy meal. The killdeer leads the fox away from the nest then flies away. The chicks wait, keeping very still and quiet until mom returns.

LIFE CYCLE FACTS

The female killdeer normally lays four eggs. The chicks hatch after about 25 days.

AMAZING BIRD LIFE CYCLE

Emperor penguin

Penguin pairs stay together for years.

Penguins cannot fly. They use their wings as flippers for swimming in the sea. Emperor penguins do not build nests. After mating, the female lays one egg. The male holds the egg on his feet to keep it warm.

The female goes off to sea to catch fish. Sometimes emperor penguins walk for more than 60 miles (100 km) to get to the sea.

All winter the male cares for the egg. In spring, the egg hatches and the female returns from the sea with food for the chick.

The new chick stays warm on the father's feet.

When the egg has hatched, the male and female take turns to care for the chick and go fishing.

Until their adult feathers grow, the chicks cannot swim. After four or five months, the chicks' feathers come in. Then they are able to go to sea to find food on their own.

The parent penguin coughs up partly digested fish for the chick.

LIFE CYCLE FACTS

The female emperor penguin lays one egg. The chick hatches after about 65 days.

Arctic tern

Arctic terns catch fish by plunging into the sea.

The Arctic tern is the champion bird traveler. Each year, this small seabird* migrates *from the Arctic to Antarctica and back again. Arctic terns fly about 22,000 miles (35,000 km) around the world every year.

Arctic terns have two summers every year.

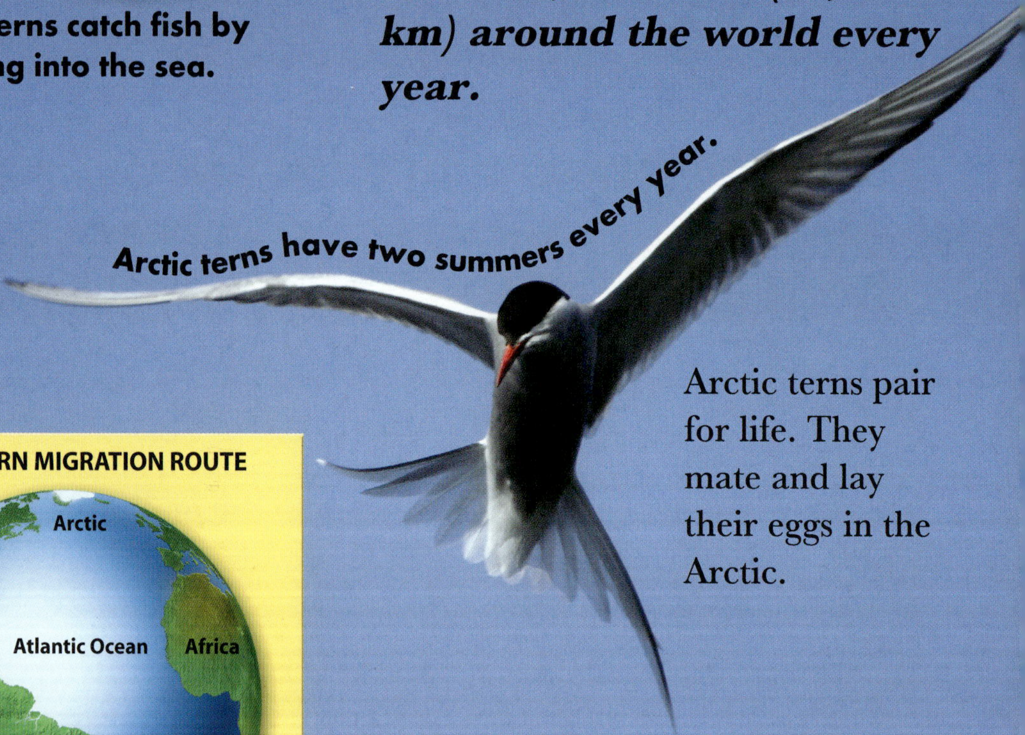

Arctic terns pair for life. They mate and lay their eggs in the Arctic.

ARCTIC TERN MIGRATION ROUTE

This map shows the Arctic tern's migration from north to south and back again.

When it is winter in the north of the world, it is summer in the south. Arctic terns fly south to escape the cold northern winter. When the southern summer ends, they fly north again.

The parent terns raise their chicks during the short Arctic summer. When it's time to fly south, the parent terns guide the youngsters to show them the way.

LIFE CYCLE FACTS

The female Arctic tern lays two or three eggs. The chicks hatch after about 24 days.

Bower bird

The satin bower bird has blue-black feathers and bright blue eyes.

Bower birds live in Australia and New Guinea. The male makes a little archway, called a bower, to attract a mate. He puts colorful things such as stones, bones, feathers, or shells inside the bower. He makes a garden too!

This is a pair of great bower birds.

After mating, the female bower bird makes a saucer-shaped nest for her eggs. The male doesn't help—he is more interested in his bower.

The male dances in and out of his bower. Females visit several bowers before deciding on a mate.

Sometimes males steal decorations from each other's bowers!

LIFE CYCLE FACTS

The female satin bower bird lays two or three eggs. The chicks hatch between 15 and 30 days later.

Satin bower birds like blue. A male may collect blue drinking straws, bits of blue plastic, and even ballpoint pens!

Tailorbird

The tailorbird lives in south Asia. It makes a very unusual nest! Just as a tailor sews cloth to make clothes, the tailorbird sews leaves together to make a nest.

Tailorbirds don't mind people. Some nest in gardens.

For thread to make their nest the bird uses plant fibres or spider's web. It makes neat, tight stitches.

Inside the leaf-bag, the bird makes a cozy nest of spider's web, bits of string—anything soft.

The tailorbird chooses a long, wide leaf. Using its beak as a needle, it sews the edges of the leaf together to make a bag shape.

The female sits on the eggs to incubate them. Both parents feed the chicks, insects and spiders.

LIFE CYCLE FACTS

The female tailorbird lays between three and five eggs. The chicks hatch after 12 days.

AMAZING BIRD LIFE CYCLE

Puffin

Puffins eat fish—they can carry 10 small fish sideways in their beaks.

The puffin is a seabird that nests on cliffs. Puffins are excellent swimmers. Male and female puffins do a courtship dance—they bob heads and touch beaks. Then they mate out at sea.

LIFE CYCLE FACTS

The female puffin lays one egg. The chick hatches after about 40 days.

The puffin pair dig a nest **burrow**, using their beaks and feet. Some puffins nest inside empty rabbit holes.

Inside the burrow, the female lays one egg. Both parents incubate the egg and catch fish for the chick when it hatches.

When the chick is six weeks old, the parents leave it. After a week on its own, the chick leaves the burrow.

The chick rushes to the sea, usually at night when there are fewer predators around. Rats and seagulls will kill puffin chicks.

Swallows stick their nests to houses or cave walls, using their gummy spit as glue.

That's amazing!

Birds are very good parents. They care for their eggs and chicks by building them a safe, cozy home and bringing them food. But did you know that there is one bird that's a very lazy parent?!

AMAZING BIRD FACT

Ostrich chicks are looked after by their dad—mom doesn't help at all!

The cuckoo lays its egg in the nest of another bird and then leaves it. The other bird does not notice the strange egg. The cuckoo chick (right) hatches after 12 days and pushes the other eggs or chicks out of the nest.

Ostrich egg

Chicken egg

An ostrich egg is the biggest egg in the bird kingdom. A hummingbird's egg is the smallest—it's about the size of a pea!

African weaver birds nest in colonies. Each pair of birds weaves a nest from grass and leaves.

Glossary

ancestors – parents, grandparents, great-grandparents—all the earlier individuals that came before

breed – to mate and have babies.

burrow – tunnels and holes under the ground where some animals live

camouflaged – having colors, marks or a shape that hides an animal from predators, and its prey

colonies – large groups

endothermic – animals whose body temperature stays the same no matter how hot or cold the air or water is around them. Humans are endothermic!

hatch – when a baby bird or animal breaks out of its egg

hollow – something empty inside

incubation – keeping an egg warm after laying and before it hatches

mammals – endothermic animals with hair, that feed their babies milk

mate – when a male and female animal meet and have babies

migrates – travels a long way to find food or a place to breed

predators – animals which hunt and kill other animals for food

rainforests – forests of tall trees in warm places with lots of rain

reptiles – animals with scales such as snakes, lizards and crocodiles

stages – different times of an animal's life when the animal changes

territory – an area or place where an animal feeds and breeds

wingspan – the distance from the tip of one wing to the tip of the other

Index

Picture credits

Shutterstock. 1: Maya Afzaa. 2-3: Stu Shaw. 4-5: Anthony Smith, Petr Jilek, Daimond Shutter, Ondrej Prosicky, Semue85. 6-7: Jeroen Mikkers, Mario Wong Pastor, Piotrek Golemo, Gaearon Tolon. 8-9: John Carnemolla, Edwin Butter, Don Mammoser, Mark Sully, Sokolov Alexey, James WIldlifeWorld. 10-11: Konstranttin, Iakov Filimonov, JT Platt, Fominayaphoto. 12-13: Mark Bridger, val Lawless, Sander van der Werf, Neil Burton, Kgrif. 14-15: Bildagentur Zoonar GmbH, Andrea J Smith, LisaCarter, Chgeryl E Davis, Gabrielle Hovey, Mike Truchon, JamesFArlkeyPhotos, Tony Campbell, Clarst5. 16-17: Kristof Bellens, MK Photograph55, JT Platt, Red ivory. 18-19: Julio Salgado, Brett Hondow, Phil Lowe, LisaCarter, FotoRequest. 20-21: Leksele, vladsilver, Sergey 402, Mario_Hoppmann. 22-23: Tony Brindley, Anders Stoustrup, AndreAnita. 24-25: Huigh Lansdown, John Carnemolla, Luke Shelley. 26-27: Vinod Pillai, Kritchai7752. 28-29: Rudmer Zwerver, LouieLea, P J Photography, Dan Bagur. 30-31: Olexander Panchenko, Jiri Hera, Dmussman, Vishnevskiy Vasily, Rich Careyow23, Rudmer Zwerver, Heather Lucia Snow, Kuttelvaserov Stuchelova, Anna_Polyakova.